WITH HEY, HO...
AND
THE MAN WITH THE SPATS

By the same Author:

Novels

THE MASK
THE WALL
BABEL
THE NEW CANDIDE
MIRANDA MASTERS
O'FLAHERTY THE GREAT
THE DEVIL IS AN ENGLISH GENTLEMAN
etc., etc.

Biography

THE MODERN PLUTARCH
AUTOBIOGRAPHY

Plays

SPORTS OF GODS
SHYLOCK'S CHOICE

Public Affairs

AN OPEN LETTER TO JEWS AND CHRISTIANS

Juvenile

A BOY NAMED JOHN
etc., etc., etc.

WITH HEY, HO...
AND
THE MAN WITH THE SPATS

by

JOHN COURNOS

ASTRA BOOKS 1963
NEW YORK

© *Copyright, 1963, by Astra Books*

Library of Congress Catalog Card Number: 63-19370

FIRST EDITION

With Hey, Ho . . . and *The Man With the Spats* includes a special edition of 50 copies, numbered and signed by the author.

ASTRA BOOKS, NEW YORK

Distributed by Twayne Publishers, Inc.
31 Union Square West, New York 3, N. Y.

PRINTED IN THE UNITED STATES OF AMERICA

CONTENTS

WITH HEY, HO . . .

Dedication: Aida ... 9

EXPERIMENTS IN CADENCE

I Loved Thee in Aforetime . . . 11
'Mid Frenzied Gale . . . 12
As the Gentle Sun . . . 12
Pavane 13
Not All Loss 13
Orpheus 14
What Price the Moon? 15
Hamlet 1960 16
A Thought for the Day 17
Debby 18
I Sit, and Listen 19
Shakespeare 20
The Sculptor and His Model 21
A Ship Went Down 22
Dream—and Reality 24
Medici Chapel, Florence 26
Poems—and Poems 27
Cassandra, Thou Art My Sister . . . 28
Last Meeting With D. H. Lawrence 29
Sherwood Anderson 30

RHYMED INTERLUDES

Plaint of An Anti-Intellectual 31
Folk Ballad 32
A Valentine 33
The Glow of Youth 34
Catherine Takes a Stroll 35
From Zero to Zero? 36

Good Intentions in Poor Rhyme	38
Hiroshima	39
New Orleans 1960	40
Merrie England 1959	40
Frustration	41
End to Innocence	42
Dirge	47
Four Months After	47
Someone Stands Outside My Door . . .	48
Danse Macabre: a Fantasia	48

SPARKS FROM THE ANVIL

"Human, All Too Human"	49
Theme for Nocturne	49
Attention: Society of Prevention of Cruelty to Old Men	49
Poor Oedipus	50
Abe Lincoln	50
Wine, Water and Tears	50
Beethoven's *Seventh Symphony*	51
Just Grin and Bear It	51
Fair Exchange	51
Diffidence	52
To a Certain Editor	52
Enough to Make One Laugh	53
His Error	53
Where Is Thy Sting?	53
Dialogue	54
Chasing One's Own Tail	54
The Berlin Wall	55
The Magic Ink-well	56
LINCOLN!	57
THE MAN WITH THE SPATS	73
"The End Is My Beginning"	123

WITH HEY, HO . . .

VENTURES INTO

CADENCE AND RHYME

DEDICATION:

AIDA

I FIRST BEHELD thy image on old Greek urn,
Fluid of line, thy form toward me did turn,
A vision thou wert in graceful stance,
Poised to join in rhythmic dance.
Thou stood out clear—ebon black on amber,
Of a sudden thou leapt into my chamber,
Thy loose draperies all aswirl,
Embracing me in one wild whirl.

How shall I thee, Aida, greet?
How shall I thine ancient spirit meet?
Should I laugh, or weep, or smile?
Should I with worship thee beguile?
Should I invoke an old elusive melody,
Or chant a resurrected threnody,
A tune salvaged from long-banked fire?
Gone, alas, the blithe days of lute and lyre.

EXPERIMENTS IN CADENCE

I Loved Thee in Aforetime

I LOVED THEE in aforetime;
Came Lethe, cast spell upon me.
I slept countless years,
An eventless dreamless sleep,
Unremembered . . .
Today to wake, my gaze upon thy face,
Serene brown eyes smiling
'Twixt smooth strands of hair,
Olive black, luminous
In light of Mediterranean sun.

'Mid Frenzied Gale

'Mid frenzied gale,
'Mid roar and moan,
'Mid pandemonium
Of writhen seas,
Of elements run amok,
You are the slender spar
To which I with ardor cling.
As wave trails wave,
As crest to crest I ride,
Rising and falling,
I cleave to you
With desperate clutch
In fear I may let go
And be swallowed
And absorbed
In mad welter
Of gathered wrath
Of deposed daimons
And anguished gods.

As the Gentle Sun

As the gentle sun illumes the serene smooth sea
So a smile serene and sweet graces her face in sleep;
As dulled daylight under cloud whips up the sea in furrows
So ill fortune from without shapes her face into tragic mask

Pavane

As I TREAD the forest path
Amid trees bare of verdure,
Bereft of fragrance,
The garrulous leaves of Fall
With loud malice crunch under foot,
Taunt me with memory of green aforetime,
When in the self-same path,
In quest of shelter from June sun,
I had walked hand in hand with Sylvia,
Moss soft under foot,
Hearts one in wordless song
Audible in deep silence
Unbroken save by tender murmur
In the tree-tops,
Pliant, swaying in rhythm,
Echoing our love.

Not All Loss

OH THE SILKEN FEEL
Of a woman's fingers
On the head in her lap
As she pulls wool
Over her lover's eyes!

Orpheus

THE WORLD JOINED in loud lament
As, his lyre singing,
He passed by,
A tragic figure with faltering gait
Forgot by Lethe
Who made forgetfulness a blessing,
And, heads bowed,
Men and women
Made his utter woe
Their own,
And lovelorn maidens,
Strewing roses,
Flung themselves in his path,
While he, unheeding,
Passing on,
Toward doom, ultimate and cruel,
Touched the strings of his lyre
With tender fingers,
And wrought music
Made magic by abysmal grief,
Its melodious echoes,
Reverberating,
Audible to this day
With unabated resonance.

What Price the Moon?

UP SPED
the Russian Lunik
toward the indifferent moon.
There was rejoicing below.

Below also,
in the Soviet Eden,
in a hovel,
a weeping mother,
her weary body
bent over ailing babe,
in prolonged agony
of patience spent,
sat waiting
for the doctor
who had been sent for
hours before . . .
She could scarcely know
he was sitting in a café
over vodka
celebrating
Lunik's journey
toward the cool Moon.

Hamlet 1960

IN PENUMBRAL LIGHT of dawn
I spied a human form
Towering immense
Loom on the horizon.
I watched him emerge,
Slowly ascend
From darkling sea.
I thought him Hamlet,
Swelling in size as he rose,
A giant figure,
His long black cloak
Draped round his shoulders,
Falling in voluminous folds,
Downward . . .
Flanked as by mountains
By two purplish clouds
Charged with thunder,
He stood on twilit shore,
Peering at the gap,
Ever widening,
Beneath his feet,
Like a vast grave . . .
He barely stirred,
So rapt in thought he seemed—
A more tragic gesture I'd never seen.
In one hand he held a roundish object
He gently fondled . . .
A skull I thought,
Doubtless Yorick's . . .
Then—suddenly—
From lowry heavens,
A shaft of blinding light
Streaked through the half-dusk,
Pierced the landscape,

Clove it in two.
I heard him heave a sigh,
I heard him murmur,
"The great orb itself . . .
Shall dissolve . . .
Leave not a rack behind . . ."
Then—suddenly—
I understood, I knew . . .
His hand held a bomb,
An A-Bomb I thought . . .
His tall form shook,
His voice trembled,
I heard him murmur . . .
"To be, or not to be . . ."
Again I heard him murmur . . .
"To be, or not to be . . ."

A Thought for the Day

AT INFINITE COST
Men dream
Of flying to the moon;
Women are wise
To greet the moonlight
And rest content.

Debby

SPRINGING from wild womb of the Caribbean,
Bearing no family likeness to remote modest cousin Venus
Gently risen, unashamedly naked, on giant oyster shell from
        tideless Mediterranean
Aptly called *thalassah* by the soft-spoken Greeks,
You, Debby, fully attired yet indecent hussy,
Lewd in skirt and petticoat tempestuously beruffled
And in lace-frilled pantaloons, and gaudy garters,
Lacking all decorum, like a slut in old-fashioned vaudeville
Following in wake of no less ill-begotten sisters,
Shameless Adele, reckless Betsy, loveless Cora,
Fathered in elemental fury by raging sea monster,
You came frisking along the Atlantic shore,
Kicking up strident propellant limbs,
Flaunting prodigal underwear
In stormy disarray of ribbon, lace and frill,
The waters recoiling in billowing broken waves,
The skirt's hems flinging up spray and foam,
Your precipitate onward rush
Forcing sturdy ships to toss along its fringes,
Making heroes of men ill-caught in havoc-stricken path.

I Sit, and Listen . . .

I sit, and listen . . .
The violins moan-groan
In lingering monotone.
They sing their lament,
Their melody lachrymose,
They sing, they sigh, they sob.
To their wordless rhythms
The pulses throb.
Now with soft sibillance
The heart-strings weep:
Then, *volte-face*, they laugh and leap.
Teeming memories
Swarming out of the past,
Out of forgotten caverns of time,
Dance . . . and, circling, wildly whirl.
Embers, long since thought dead,
Catch flame, flare a fiery red,
Fill soul with molten solace,
An alchemy that makes refulgent gold
Out of sodden lead.
Keen joy, exquisite pain,
Mingle as April sun with rain . . .
I sit intent and listen, listen
To overtones and undertones
Of love and dread,
The soul's wine, the soul's bread . . .
The contrapuntal melody
Runs through the blood,
The ineffable surge
Of tremulous melancholy
Comes hurtling in a flood,
Drowning pettiness and dross,
Oblivious of gain and loss,
The fortissimo is silence,
Silence . . .
Sonorous, and eloquent, and deep.

Shakespeare

O SHAKESPEARE!
Bard without peer,
To poets a despair
And a spur,
The world adores you,
Yet has learned naught
From life's spectacle
Faithfully rendered
On your several stages . . .
O Shakespeare,
England's incomparable gift
To a world which so often
Reviles the giver
Oblivious of the truth:
He who reviles England
Reviles you.

The Sculptor and His Model

A CURVED WHITE SHIP comes not more white
Out of darkness
Than you came out of your wine-dark robe.

Your flowing garment fell away from you softly,
Lay about you,
A heap of petals clinging to a snow-white stalk.

When my eyes beheld you so tall, so white,
Your head drooping,
Thoughts of kisses retreated quickly to their nest.

For my eyes beheld you, a white statue,
With enchantment,
My firm clear eyes held back the lover's heart.

A Ship Went Down

The other day I read of an old ship
Which, in dead calm of serene day,
Within sight of port,
Within sight of bystanders,
Foundered—with precious cargo.

For three score years and ten,
This ship, the *Wayfarer*,
Had trafficked
Between ports of Seven Seas,
Pausing now at isles of loveliness,
Now in tangled jungles of nameless pain,
There to gather fresh treasure
At cost of love's labor
And infinite patience.

Within the secret recesses of this ship,
In sinuous compartments,
Hidden gems of worth cunningly reposed,
Precious jade, and pearls, and opals,
Of so rare a quality as to have no peer.

Yet exceeding odd it was
That no one wished to see them,
No one thought gifts worth while
Which were not for sale,
To be had for the asking.
Suspicious eyes, under raised eyebrows,
Looked askance, turned their attention
To costume jewelry in shop windows
On Fifth Avenue.

The Captain of the ship,
A worthy fellow, serene in manner,
Had once let me have a glimpse
Of a few of his treasures.
I felt entranced
As by a finger touching
A tiny opal of rare luster
A diffusive gentle glow
Stole through the branching paths
Of the unseen network of my being,
Reaching the brain,
Where for an instant
It seemed to flare,
Leaving me suffused
With longing for beauty
Almost too great to bear.
I promised to return—
I never did.

The old hulk of the ship went down.
I read of it in the "Obits" of *The Times*,
Which prints only news "fit to print"
And misses nothing . . .
In a few lines it told of the death
And of the ripples which lingered briefly
After the old ship went down.
The Captain had no known kin,
There were no services,
No prayers for the dead,
None to mourn, or shed a tear.

Dream—and Reality

BEFORE YOU WERE BORN,
Transcendent image in mind
I loved you ...
In vain endeavor,
Questing this way and that,
I sought you ...
In the hurly-burly of life,
Mad phantasmagoria of being,
I forgot you ...

Tonight—
As I was fleeing,
Hot on my heels
Pursuing shadows,
Multiple ghosts of vanished years,
By chance I glimpsed you
In the flesh,
Dancing, dancing ...
In Minoan bell-like skirt
Of aforetime,
Circling, dancing,
Swaying to Life's heady rhythm
With elusive grace,
Evoking memories ...
I saw you
As in shadow-play,
Tremulous in light penumbral,
Against drop-curtain
Of wavering drapery,
Dancing ... swaying ...
Calling forth a vision
Of the long forgotten,
The suddenly remembered ...
To haunting lilting tune,

Taunting melody . . .
The siren song of Maya . . .
Receding into distance . . . fading . . .
Trailing in wake
A pervasive aroma
Of nostalgic lament
And ineffable regret . . .

"Awake! Awake!"
Hand to shoulder someone shook me,
Roughly nudged me . .
"This, the *World's End*,
Night club for night people,
Is no place for slumber . . .
Here come the girl herself,
The dancer . . .
She'd like a drink!"
I rubbed my eyes . . .
I saw a bepainted slut,
Smile akin to grin,
Ugly and obscene . . .
Heard, in voice raucous, say . . .
"Want me, darling?"

What trespass in aforetime,
What forgot transgression,
What vengeful fury,
Has decreed this compulsive agony,
This torment of youth remembered,
This reluctant propulsion
To dubious shelter
Of irremediable reality
Of inescapable everydayness:
The abiding tyranny
Of Common Sense?

Medici Chapel, Florence

BAEDECKER IN HAND,
A woman went in,
Stayed five minutes,
Came out.
To her friend,
Who remained outside,
She said with glee:
"Why, my dear,
I simply had to see it,
It's four-starred,
It's a 'must'!"

Clean,
Immaculately groomed,
A man went in,
Stayed an hour,
Came out,
Rapt in thought.
He said nothing
To his friend
Who waited at the café.
It was his friend who spoke:
"Why are your trousers rumpled?
Why dust on your knees?"

Poems—and Poems

I KNEW A POETESS,
Tall and handsome,
With sexy eyes,
Who aspired
To be sister to Sappho.
She was much admired
For her iambics—
And hexameters,
And was a cult
Among the dilettanti.

One evening
Over a restaurant table
She pulled a slip of paper
From her handbag.
Flaunting it,
She said—
A warm glint in her eyes,—
"Here is a poem—
The most beautiful in the world!"
Eagerly, I looked.
It was a cheque—
For Fifty Pounds!
Signed by an art patron.

Cassandra, Thou Art My Sister . . .

Cassandra, thou art my sister . . .
Apollo had conferred on thee
The unasked-for gift of prophecy
With the odious purpose
Of propitiating thee
To become his bedfellow.
Then . . . he the male scorned . . . petulant,
Unable to retract his gift,
Put a curse on it:
Thou were bereft of power to inspire belief.
It was a caddish thing to do,
No gentleman would stoop
To do so vile a thing to fair lady.

Cassandra, thou are my sister . . .
My gift is no less accursed.
Speak fervently as I might,
With the eloquence of truth,
No one will listen.
So I follow the way of prophets,
Lifting my voice in the wilderness,
Where God doth look on, and smile,
While vultures soar overhead,
Avidly scan the earth,
Awaiting that which is not yet here
But which in good time is sure to come . . .
The vultures have faith.

Last Meeting With D. H. Lawrence

It was in the mid-twenties ...
We—Helen and I—
And you, Lawrence,
Sat in a Florence café,
At the time of a Fascisti Festival.
You were benign
As you paid a compliment to Helen.
And you began to speak
Of a nice island somewhere ...
You were interrupted
By the Fascisti
Who insisted that all rise
To share in a toast
To Benito Mussolini,
Of whom we usually spoke as "Mr. Jones."
It was harmless,
We were not fools,
We rose to our feet.
Then—after the toast—
We sat down again.
And you, Lawrence,
Resumed where you left off:
"Yes, it would be nice,
For folks like us,
To find an island,
And form a small colony
Where we could live together
As people should live,
Untroubled by either rabble
Or whited sepulchres ..."

Sherwood Anderson

OF SHERWOOD!
Friend of friends,
Alas, no longer among the living,
Yet living abundantly for me
In letter you once wrote me.
Did I say letter?
No, not letter,
But pulsating parchment
Of understanding
And touching tenderness
Rekindled now at thought of it
And by memory
Of warmth in your eyes
And welcoming gesture
At each meeting . . .
Thought of that letter
Is as thought of living fire in grate
Over which I spread my hands
To receive warmth,
Greater warmth,
From you, unhappily dead,
Than from those among the living,
However hard they grasp my hand in theirs
And swear eternal fealty and friendship . . .

December 1962

RHYMED INTERLUDES

Plaint of An Anti-intellectual

Buddha and Mahomet and Rameses the Great
Have put their heads together to administer my fate.

Plato and Socrates and all-knowing Aristotle
Are intent on feeding me the bottle.

My education, say the Commies, will not be complete
Until I have sat for years at Karl Marx's feet.

William James, Santayana, John Dewey too,
The day I met them is the day I rue.

A thousand learned sages are sitting on my chest,
By the weight of their wisdom my soul is oppres't.

If "a little knowledge is a dangerous thing"
Just think how much peril much knowledge can bring.

So much to have learned, so much to forget,
If I study any longer I'll land in Bedlam yet.

So I'll go to Marseilles and play with the girls,
And extract what lore may be entangled in curls.

Or join the chimpanzees, hop from tree to tree,
If that's the way to Wisdom I shall be free.

I must make up my mind as to which it shall be,
That shouldn't be too hard, for I have my Ph.D.

Folk Ballad

My love, my love has gone away,
To sail over the briny sea.
I pine by night, I pray by day,
Will my love e'er come back to me?

My love, my love has gone away,
Afar I peer athwart cruel sea.
No sight of sail, no light of ray,
Will my love e'er come back to me?

My love, my love has gone away,
Into the surf I let fall a tear.
The wave sings on its ruthless lay,
Oh, if only my love were near!

My love, my love has gone away,
Each day I scan the writhen sea,
My arms outspread I wordless pray,
If only my love would come back to me!

A Valentine
To——

I AM three score—and twenty,
So what's to be done, my dear?
I must resign love's plenty
And say my prayers, I fear.

Too bad so late I met you,
Too late for love, my sweet,
If I were only twenty-two
I'd wed you *tout de suite*.

I've gathered aged wisdom,
Surfeit of sense and lore,
But I'd give away my kingdom
To be only twenty-four!

The Glow of Youth
(For S.C.)

Outdoors the endless rain,
Within—pervasive gloom,
On entering the room
You exorcised the pain.

From Eire so fair a rose,
Soft sheen aglow with light
To grant the heart delight,
To confer on mind repose.

And may you come again
For brief spell to enlull
Chaos of warring soul,
Glow not afar in vain!

Catherine Takes a Stroll

SHE HURRIES . . .
Her life is one long Marathon.
She tarries . . .
Only to put something pretty on.

Never still,
She hastens this way, then that,
Up steep hill:
To get to top as quick as scat.

Once there,
She'll not think it time to stop.
Sans care
She'll scamper down, then—what else but up?

Another mile!
The Angels must love to see her run,
They smile:
To see her speeding is such fun!

The wind stirs:
She creates breezes when she walks.
The wind purrs:
Grows gentle when she stops and talks.

From Zero to Zero?

W E'D EMERGED from a door the shape of Zero
In a state as amoral as of fiddling Nero,

We moved along in endless queue,
All in all we were quite a few.

We trudged on slowly viewing the sights,
Seeing people perform the oddest rites.

Ominous loomed another Zero ahead,
As we drew near, reluctant grew our tread.

We entered the door with a quaking qualm,
Intoning chants to induce craved balm.

Some cursed, some said their prayers,
Some laid aside their daily cares.

Some felt in a blessed state of grace
Some wondered how to save their face.

Shrieks mingled with joys unalloyed,
Some felt happy, more felt destroyed.

'Twas then I awake from my evil dream,
I drank some coffee minus the cream.

I told my dream to a Freudian friend,
From ear to ear the silly ass grinned.

"The dream was perfect," he said with a smirk,
"A true demonstration of the Oedipus quirk.

"You sought to escape from dear mamma's womb,
Only to find refuge in the womb-like tomb.

"From Zero to Zero is Life's true rule,
That must be clear to an arrant fool.

"From nothingness to nothingness we go on,
Bequeathing like fate from father to son."

I was angry with my friend for so gross a libel:
"You'll find nothing like that in the Holy Bible!"

Good Intentions in Poor Rhyme

Sans reason or rhyme
She spent her time
In hopeless quest
Of own home nest.

From friend to friend she went,
They thought her heaven-sent;
Yet she'd have loved to lay her head
In her own, her very own bed.

May God confer a little space
Upon this lady of sweet grace
That she may find surcease
In this hapless quest for peace.

Hiroshima

(for Edita Morris)

'Tis LONG past midnight, I fain would sleep;
In vain I'd counted ten thousand sheep.
With each instant I grow more wide awake;
'T'has naught to do with aught for conscience' sake.

I feel mute memories coursing through the blood
Well nigh forgot, they surge in turgid flood.
Inarticulate, blind, they elude my grasp.
At point of contact, they escape my ardent clasp.

Can it be the city I'd long since seen laid waste
By men who had acted in oh so breathless haste?
Terrible the cruel onslaught of human wrath
Yet I had seen the city only in the aftermath.

Lucky they who unaware met merciful release,
Hapless the blighted remnant who coveted their peace.
Theirs to endure unremitting ache and pain,
To suffer in racking fear lest they go insane.

What men do to men is absurdly, madly tragic;
Once done, to undo their deeds there is no magic.
No pity can atone for woes of stricken city,
By far the greater pity is: there is no pity.

New Orleans 1960

NOT TO LEAVE Jesus in the lurch
On Sundays folks all go to church.
Week days, when they see a Negro child,
With inflamed fury they go wild.
How dare a wee black girl invade their school?
Such thought ne'er entered the mind of fool.
In mobs they gather to protect their pride,
They hardly know they're Jekyll and Hyde.
The wee black girl has heart in mouth,
Poor thing, to face the gallant South,
Pursued by howls and snarls, to brave the storm,
To run mad gauntlet to reach her form.

Merrie England 1959

(It Really Happened)

THERE WAS A BRITON who lived in a tree,
The Law came along, said it cannot be.
He'd have to move for sake of decency
(This is of no concern to you or to me).
But "Britons never shall be slaves...."
(Besides, just think of the money it saves!)
"Officer, you must be a real donkey
To think I may do less than a monkey!"
So the matter was duly taken to Court,
Verdict: an Englishman's tree was his fort!

Frustration

All evening long last night
I waited for a bus.
Other people stood beside,
None made a fuss.

In vain I sought a taxi,
No taxi was in sight.
The others stood in dead huddle,
It was a moonless night.

I thought of those in fret at home,
It was near dead of night.
Nowhere could I find a phone,
Nor shadow of life in sight.

One woman sprang into life,
Jumped on a passing truck.
I wished I'd done the same,
I tried but had no luck.

We thought it a coming bus
Each time we saw a light,
It proved a false alarm,
Endless seemed the night.

Hope flared at each nearing light,
Always a false alarm.
Hope flared, hope died,
I wished myself on a farm.

At last the wished-for bus,
Helpless, without a brake,
Rushed headlong toward me.
With a cry I came awake.

End to Innocence

One morn when Adam did awake
And thought his burning thirst to slake
He found a strange creature at his side.
"Hey, ho, what's this!" he loudly cried,
As his eyes with joy did alight
With fresh-sprung pleasure at the sight.

He could not understand the unbidden shiver
As his limbs against hers did gently quiver.
How very odd, he thought: she's all curve,
What purpose was it meant to serve?

The rounded landscape of her frame,
As yet he had for it no name.
Presences and lacks, too, there were,
Odd yet acting as a peculiar spur
To sensations wholly fresh
As flesh encountered flesh.

When she oped her azure eyes
To delight him, and surprise.
Her gaze upon him was intent,
And loving, truly heaven-sent.

Soft fingers his contours did caress,
Her eyes all-knowing under fair tress.
To her overtures he responded
With a joy quite unbounded.
She pressed against him like a kitten,
Mysteriously he felt smitten.

It ended as such things should end,
Her head lay in his shoulder bend,
He stroking her so silken hair,
Its texture soft, its sheen so rare.

Said he, suddenly arising
With an alacrity surprising:
"Let's slake our thirst at the cool spring
And let our voices go ting-a-ling!"
He pulled her up, in her eyes no shame,
As yet for this they had no name.

Hand in hand, both lad and lass
Barefoot trod soft upon the grass,
Until they came to the guilty tree
Which was to end their jubilee.

God had spoken with a warning breath:
To eat of its fruit might lead to death.
The fruit thereof was fair to behold,
They wished of its evil they'd not been told.

They stood before the tree, its fruit admired,
Poor innocents, their temptations fired.
Fruit surely was made to be consumed,
What other purpose could be presumed?

A leering serpent round the tree entwined
Whispered subtly into the woman's mind.
A grin in his green crafty eyes,
He murmured: "Eat the apple and be wise.
They're ripe, and good to the taste,
Why allow them to go to waste?"

Forthwith the woman thus beguiled
Plucked an apple and at Adam smiled.
"Here, my dear, take thou the primal bite!"
He did: his eyes of a sudden did alight.

To his eyes' challenge she did respond,
Of a sudden of him she grew more fond.
She'd covered his bite with her very own,
Unaware of the new life they had sown.

He gazed at her in fresh surprise,
Found a new tenderness in her eyes.
She turned her eyes away, demure;
She loved him, of that he now was sure.

"I'd not known thou wert so fair," he said.
"And thou so strong and fair," she echoed.
They gazed at each other in comprehension,
Both fired with a mounting tension.

Hand in hand, they came to a tree,
Released from some enchantment, and now free.
She ran, o'er shoulder begging to be caught;
It was a chase with pleasure fraught.

A flush like a sunrise suffused her face
As Adam flung out an arm her to embrace.
She fled from him to a tree with figs abounding,
To snatch at leaves from breezes grounding.

She made them aprons from leaves so green,
To cover up what were best unseen.
They'd discovered the thing called shame
It made love a more thrilling game.

Alas, alas! There's an end to rapture,
Moments will come for its recapture,
But for the present life bids woe,
Alas, alas! Were it not so!

Just then from a grove over yonder
Came a voice the sound of thunder:
"Adam, Adam, where art thou?
I have sought thee high and low!"

"I'd made no answer," Adam replied,
"For, being naked, I could scarce abide
Being seen, without shame,
Lacking a garment to my name!"
His voice had lost its primal lilt,
It rich-bespoke a sense of guilt.

"Naked, Adam? Who told you this?
How coulds't thou apparel miss
Unless forbidden fruit did ope thine eyes
To what is foolish, and to what is wise?"

"The woman urged me to take a bite,
My eyes were opened to wrong and right,
To keen pain, and keener pleasure,
Aware am I now of my own measure."

Poor man! Bemused, thus Eve to blame.
Fore'er it would remain the same.
In time to come it would ne'er be Adam,
The fault would always lie with Madam!

"Adam, when thus thou opened they eyes,
Thou lost they right to Paradise.
Hence out thou'll go to meet toil and woe,
Evermore to contend with soil and foe."

Wrathful Adonai now turned to Eve,
"For what thou did thou shalt ever grieve!"
"The serpent beguiled me!" she did say.
For his counsel I now must pay!"

"Accursed be thou, on thy belly crawl,
With his heel man thy head shall maul,
And thou in turn shall bite his heel,
For eternity both fierce hate shall feel!"

Thus to the Serpent, then to the Woman:
"Thy fate shall be the eternal human,
In pain and torment thou shalt conceive and bear,
Lone thy ordeal, which none can share.

"To thy husband thou shalt ever cleave,
Thou couldst do naught without his leave.
Thy offspring shall bring thee trouble,
Thy burden shall be ever double.

"Now lest ye pluck fruit from Tree of Life,
Thou Adam, and thou Eve, his wife,
Tarry not, go hence—from this fair garden—
Resolve ye must your wills to harden.
And Eden shall pursue you to the end—
An eternal dream your souls to rend!"

Hand in hand, together clinging,
The Lord's words in mind still ringing,
They passed shaken through the gate.
It was night—in Spring; the hour was late.

Sadly they cast a backward glance,
At the gate a Cherubim, with flaming lance.
He swung it right to left, then left to right,
Until the tragic pilgrims were out of sight.

Onward they trod toward appointed task,
An unwished-for quest they did not ask.
For their perilous adventure they did bravely brace,
Unaware of goal: creation of the human race.

Dirge

Silent I sit, silent I mourn
For her who has gone away,
From my side my love was torn,
The cherished do not stay.

She has come, she has gone,
She will not come again.
Where lie her flesh and bone
There's nought but sun and rain.

Idle to call, idle to weep,
For she has come, and gone,
Idle for sun's beams to leap,
Or for wild winds to moan.

Four Months After

When I dream,
Then awake,
It does seem
As if she spake.
I open my eyes,
I think her near.
Loath to rise,
Say: "Yes, my dear!"

Someone Stands Outside My Door . . .

SOMEONE STANDS outside my door, and waits.
As yet faintly I can hear its very breath.
He, She, or It—I cannot tell—it may be Death.
Invisible yet palpable, my very self it baits.

Should I open the door and say, "Come in!"?
"No," It says, "my presence I cannot lend,
You must live and endure unto the end."
"Why? I've lived too long—that is my sin!"

Danse Macabre: a Fantasia
(for Aida)

WHEN THE Last Visitor makes his call
With clamorous clarionets
To make of me his helpless thrall
You come too, my dear: bring your castanets,
And dance for me your wildest dance
With all your zest and skill
To put him out of countenance
And provide me with last thrill.
As I watch the impresario of death,
A leery fellow with hollow eyes,
Come to deprive me of my breath,
I shall offer him a surprise:
At last click I'll shout a loud guffaw,
Whereupon his teeth will crackle
And there'll be a gnashing of his jaw,
To accompaniment of shrill cackle.

SPARKS FROM THE ANVIL

"Human, All Too Human"
(for Ingeborg)

I LIKE TO THINK of you as Eve, Mother of Men,
Let knave and fool give thought to Sun-Yat-Sen.
Our earth is good; you can't be seen too often or too soon,
Fools they who contemplate the joy of journey to the Moon.

Theme for Nocturne

ELUSIVE NIGHT hides more than forthright day reveals,
Unseen delights, and indiscreet, with subtlety conceals
Caught unaware, flaunts guilt in Morn's incipient flush,
Without ado, blatant Daylight dissipates the blush.

Attention:
Society of Prevention of Cruelty to Old Men!

HER FATHER was old, oh so very old,
Close to ninety, or more—so I've been told.
Dry-eyed she stayed when at last he died,
When her pet cat died, she cried and cried.

Poor Oedipus

UNHAPPY Oedipus Rex,
We connect the title with sex,
'T'is really too bad,
Maybe only a fad
To reduce a proud man
To a ridiculous complex,
Symbol of maladroit sex.

Abe Lincoln

WHEN Anne Rutledge died
He had not cried;
He bore his secret in his heart
Lest his sorrow he impart
To others, he told bawdy tales
And laughed in gales.
He did this out of sheer fear
That he break and shed a tear.

Wine, Water and Tears

To GIVE joy to bridegroom and to bride,
To make them feel themselves beside,
Jesus at Cana turned water into wine.
I've heard of folks who'd turn wine into brine,
Who believe it does good to shed salt tears
By men and women beset with woe and fears;
They'd turn the Christian doctrine inside out
To gratify their strange craving to do without.

Beethoven's Seventh Symphony

RESTRAINED by gravity, earth-bound,
I gave ear to Symphony Number Seven ...
I soared, was lost in ascending sound,
I found myself borne to Seventh Heaven.

Just Grin and Bear It

NOT TO BE a mature adult
Is the fashionable cult.
Lest it drive you into a rage
Pretend you are below your age ...

❅   ❅   ❅

With appreciative mockery
Watch him shatter priceless crockery.

Fair Exchange

"LET'S SWAP our wives," he said,
"You'll find mine rather good in bed."
His mind was on his wife's sharp tongue,
The one thing he had found wrong.

"It's okay with me, brother,"
Comradely said the other.
My wife, too, is no mean slouch,
Once you get her on the couch!"
He too was thinking of her tongue,
The one thing he had found wrong.

The wives offered no objection,
They had no idea of rejection.
It would be a welcome change, they said,
'Twas far better than being dead.
Change was the law of life'd they heard,
Maybe the second would lead to third.

No sooner said than done,
It really was such jolly fun.

So the husbands swapped their wives
Only to find they'd swapped two knives.

Diffidence

You came to my door
With fire and zeal.
I paced the floor
When I wished to kneel.

To a Certain Editor

You liked me, you were my friend
When help was needed;
For this I am grateful.
Yet my song you liked not.
That song, alas, was the real me.

Enough to Make One Laugh

The world is such a funny place.
What's funnier than a rat race?
They run and squeal, and squeal and run,
To watch backbiting is such fun!

His Error

"I want to be an artist and a man,
"The two in one," he said.
Unwisely, then, he wed.
'Twas she decided, she who won.

Where Is Thy Sting?

May not humility but pride
Adorn my face when death betide,
No shame be writ on my winding sheet
Despite in fight I met defeat.
Defeat is nothing, the fight is all,
Had David's cunning vanquished Saul?

Dialogue

A. "THERE IS no ill that money will not cure!"
B. "And of that, dear sir, are you quite sure?"
A. "Just try and send some to one who is sad!"
B. "But will that cure one who is money-mad?"

Chorus in the background:
    "Money, money, money,
    Makes the world go round,
    Makes life sweet as honey,
    And a lot of sound . . .

    "If you have money to burn,
    Hell is the place,
    It will be done to a turn
    Before your face. . . .
    "Money, money, money. . . ."
              etc.

Chasing One's Own Tail

WHAT A WONDER—Automation!
A true marvel—a workless nation!
You want to work—a future carve?
You have plenty of time to starve.
Luckiest he who Robot is,
He can have his bread and cheese.
But for poor owner there's a snag,
For who'll buy and bring him swag?
Every hen her eggs still lays,
Too bad it doesn't work both ways.

The Berlin Wall

To PROTECT their House of Ill Fame
They have erected a Wall of Shame.
Their unwilling victims who work within
Are akin to White Slaves forced to sin.
The mindless eunuchs who run the place
Are cruel fools of brazen face;
Heartless, in close pact with devil,
Unaware of own dire evil.

The Magic Ink-well

SHAKESPEARE dipped in
And brought up supreme beauty
To enchant the world.

Thomas Jefferson dipped in
And brought up the Declaration
To make men free and equal.

Karl Marx dipped in
And brought up a bomb
To disrupt humanity.

Adolf Hitler dipped in
And brought up gas chambers
To asphyxiate six million Jews.

A faithful scribe dipped in
And brought up the Master's words:
"My words shall not pass away."

Whoever dips into the magic ink-well
Will bring up good or evil
According to his own desire.

Let us preserve the ink-well:
Evil dies by its own rot,
The good endures.

LINCOLN!*

To Robert Y. Gromet

1

BEHOLD!
     The man!
          Lincoln!
Man—yet more than man:
Myth,
Monument,
Soul of a people,
Incarnation of truth:
All this—
Above all a man,
A man like any man—
Of flesh and blood,
And human,
Oh so human!

2

None more sober
In grim hour
Of woe abysmal
Calling for fortitude
And endurance,
And supreme faith
In ultimate triumph
Against long night
Fraught with strife,
Savage carnage,
Seemingly endless,
Awaking despair,

---

* The last part of this poem was read by the author on T.V.—Camera Three, C.B.S., on Lincoln's Birthday, 1961. The whole poem was read three times on WBAI in 1963.

Deep and utter.
Drunken with subdued ardor
In faith in right,
He—a man of peace—
Ear cocked
For faint token
Of precious gift
His heart craved . . .
Peace . . .
His heart,
Heart of loving father,
Kindly, withal firm,
Doting on his children.
Hands hanging at sides
Limp—helpless—
To disembroil them
From mad melee
Of unflagging fratricide,
Heedless needless slaughter
To bereave
Mothers,
Wives,
Sisters,
Sweethearts,
Left to mourn
In long aftermath.

3

Heart weighted with grief,
Face graced with faint smile,
Immeasurably tragic,
Will steadfast—
Staunch against tears,
He stood there,
Human monolith,
Outwardly distraught,

Moved by compassion,
All embracing,
Beyond utterance—
Near to breaking-point,
Yet ne'er to break . . .

4

Amid seas aswirl,
Wave upon wave breaking,
The Furies singing
In mood sinister
Of disaster
Past and pending,
He stood there,
Destiny attending,
A lone figure,
Islanded,
A human lighthouse,
Lashed by adverse winds,
Frenzied rage
Of rampant elements . . .
Hurricane
Of unleashed inhuman wrath,
Savage and unsated,
Without respite
Intent on course,
Cruel and callous,
Of wrack and desolation—
And death—
Sudden, violent, premature,
To anguished chorus
Of prolonged moans
And groans
Of infernal untuneful clamor:
Unresolved antiphony
Of jangled sounds:

Blare of trumpet,
Crash of cymbals,
Rattle of kettledrums,
Joined in ultimate cacophony:
Harsh dissonance
Of warring passions
Evoked out of abysses.
Fathered by Adam,
Cain, born of Eve,
From long slumber emergent,
Bent on murder . . .
Brother against brother
In world of feral reality,
On a scale vast,
Unimaginable . . .

5

Frozenly immobile,
Seemingly serene,
Racked inwardly
With deep disquiet,
Shot through with pity,
He stood there
By tall window
Of the White House,
Peering . . . peering
Down broad avenue,
Lost in contemplation
Of things not there,
Eyes intent on landscape
Vast—boundless—
Panorama
Strewn with human anthills
And bivauc fires,
Men in huddles
Or moving in turgid masses

And straggling groups,
Silent or singing,
Minds among them
Intent on the morrow
Fraught with imaginings:
To be, or not to be . . .
He stood there,
Vision enveloping
Frightening vistas,
Realms of futile slaughter,
From Potomac to Gulf of Mexico,
From Mississippi to the sea,
Blood-drenched earth
Trod by cruel heel
Of ruthless Ares,
An impartial deity
Taking equal toll
Of all souls,
Whether Hector or Achilles,
And, on either side,
Of humble folk,
The Browns and the Joneses,
Their lot to endure
The constant threat
To home-coming
Long deferred,
Even while above their heads
By them unknowing
The cruel god's sword
Is poised to strike.

6

Then—
His position shifting—
Mindless as in a dream,
As it were, a living automaton,

Overcharged with feeling,
Moved by blind impulsion,
Hands locked behind him,
He paced up and down,
Up and down,
Up and down,
Helplessly,
With mathematical precision,
Musing upon the fates
Which made him custodian
Of a people
In hour of supreme peril ...
Then—briefly diverted—
Pondered upon what might have been:
Of gentle Ann Rutledge
Enbosomed in earth,
Of Robert,
Cut down in youth,
Of wife moody,
Afflicted with strange ailment
Alien to mind's peace,
Only to revert
To thought of his people,
The senseless slaughter,
Fructifying grief.
What a burden
In this hour,
To be human,
Oh so human!

7

Some thought you ugly ...
True, we do not see you
In imagined terms
Of sculptured Apollo.
Did Venus really rise

From foam of the sea?
Of ultimate polish none . . .
You sprang from the earth,
Out of the ruggedness of the earth,
Bits of earth still clinging . . .
Ah, but you were beautiful
In your imperfections,
In your earthy ruggedness
And artless naturalness . . .
They thought you beautiful,
The distraught mothers
Who came to see you,
To petition to save sons
Remiss in duties
On battlefield . . .
In sorrow they came,
In joy departed . . .
What they had sought
They found:
Your dedication to humanness,
To remembrance
Of the old call of the heart . . .
They were to remember
The most memorable thing about you:
You were human, *oh so human* . . .

8

Saint without halo
Clothed in soft radiance,
Penumbral—as of candlelight,
Paradoxically
Out of inner firmness
Diffusing gentleness.
Mysterious the ways of God
Who created him:
Simplicity with dignity,

Strength with sorrow,
Justice with mercy,
Charity with comprehension,
Shrewdness with integrity,
Melancholy with humor:
A miracle of wholeness.
Orator—sparing of words,
Thespian—without gesture
Or flail of arms,
Tragedian—without tears
Visible outwardly—
A face infinitely sad,
Adorned with smile.
A being whole
And wholly human,
In performance of duty
Inwardly aware
Of fate impending:
He the sacrifice,
One for the many:
Doom foreordained,
Final, irrevocable . . .

Human, oh so human,
Uniquely merciful,
Love your dialectic,
Anathema to the tyrant
Who dare not name you,
Your good his evil . . .
Your words at Gettysburg,
Symphony of sound and meaning,
Spell hope to thralls
Striving to break their chains.
Like One Other,
You could have said with truth:
"My words shall not pass away."
Down endless centuries

They will vibrate and speak,
Even as out of Time's ruins
The words of Cicero,
Slain by tyrant,
Still echo
From Roman Forum,
Today a shamble.

Oh shall we see your like again?

Your fell as a giant falls
Casting a vast frantic shadow
Athwart the land,
In the fall your long arms aflail
Grasping your children
In grief's embrace,
They too stunned to utter groan,
Or find voice in loud lament,
The ensuing silence
Audible across remote seas,
Leaving an unending trail of grief
As yet unspent . . .

Oh, Lincoln! If we ever forget you
We deserve to perish,
To vanish from the earth
Leaving no trace,
Vanish into that darkness
Of which it has been said
That "the light shineth in darkness;
And the darkness comprehended it not."

THE MAN WITH THE SPATS

A NARRATIVE POEM OF THE RUSSIAN REVOLUTION

A Word to the Reader

This narrative poem, conceived in actual experience, was [cr]eated in the most extraordinary circumstances. By no means was it a case, in Wordsworth's phrase, of "emotion remembered [in] tranquillity." On the contrary, it was the product of emotion [re]corded in emotion.

Briefly: my wife, to whom I had been married thirty-five [ye]ars, was dying after a protracted illness, resulting from a [str]oke, which left her unable to walk. During this period I was [nu]rse, shopper, cook and what not, doing my best to earn what [liv]ing I could on the side. It was not easy for her, by tempera[m]ent an active intelligent woman, to be witness to her own [ste]ady deterioration; nor for me to be a daily observer of this [un]happy process which specialists pronounced inevitable, a [pr]ocess which I was helpless to stay.

The culmination came in the last week of July, 1959 and [th]e first two weeks in August—three unforgettable hot, humid [w]eeks—during which this poem was written, in a mood of mental [ag]ony, sleeplessness and intolerable fatigue, overcome only [th]rough the unlooked-for and wholly strange emergence of the [w]ill, whose very impact with these factors seemed to create the [de]sperate energy which produced the poem. Intended in the [fir]st place to be only two or three pages, in the working the [th]eme ran away with the author so that in the end it came to [si]xty-six typed pages.

However, I am not making a plea for the poem on the purely [pe]rsonal factors which went to its making, but on its intrinsic [w]orth, and its significance in our own time.

Not only does it portray a single day in the history of the [R]ussian Revolution, but it delves into the past which brought it [ab]out, and, what is more important, looks into the future, with [th]e potential rise of a billion-headed China, a Frankenstein [cr]eated by Communist Russia, a monster who with the cruel [fa]talism of the Mongol will have little scruple in making use

69

of the nuclear weapons of the West, probably, ironically enough, by beginning with Russia herself, her mentor. Indeed, it was only two or three years ago that Mao declared that in any ensuing conflict China could easily spare three hundred million of her own people in the mad quest for power.

Genghis Khan's Golden Hordes had over-run Russia once before. This time Genghis Khan will have Karl Marx for ally. It is rather odd that no one has ever mentioned the fact that in Russia and other civil wars, Marx has already caused far more deaths than that loathsome monster, Adolf Hitler. It is odd, too, that Lenin should be held with such reverence by many Westerns. Is it so easy to forget that he was a man who could speak of human beings in terms of eggs to be beaten into an omelet? Let us be realistic, and admit that, in some respects, he was a great man, in others he was little short of a scoundrel. Hitler copied him in his espousal of the propaganda value of the whopping big lie, so zealously adhered to today by peace-loving Nikita.

There are indications that Soviet Russia's prodigious pupil, China, is outgrowing her mentor. It is a possible irony that it is precisely Soviet Russia that may be the first to suffer from an invasion of the Mongols. Is it not, indeed, for this reason that Khrushchev is chary of supplying China with nuclear arms? And let us by all means ponder on Napoleon's words: "Let China sleep. When she awakens the world will be sorry!"

Such is the theme of *The Man with the Spats*. Those who want a realistic story will find it here also. The memory of the man has persisted through forty-four years and has demanded expression.

There is but this to add. The style in which the poem is written came naturally, hammered out in the process of writing. I could think of no other method that would have answered the purpose. The interpollation of the imaginary conversation between Genghis Khan and Karl Marx before the statue of the Bronze Horseman in Petrograd, rendered in prose, is the sole exception. Here, too, however, the author has sought to express ideas in a way that the so-called average man may understand.

July 1960

JOHN COURNOS

Poetry is the spontaneous overflow of powerful feelings: it takes its origin from emotion recollected in tranquillity.
—WORDSWORTH

It also happens sometimes that it is emotion recollected in emotion.
—THE AUTHOR

Proem

Those of you who've read
The book about ten days
That shook John Reed
And caused him to deplore old ways
Should take a look at facts
And read about the evil acts
Of men who think it lots of fun
To "wash a brain" with rack and gun
And drown it in a bloody bath
To gratify their petty wrath.
If you are very fond of gore
You'll read this and ask for more.
What follows I've seen with mine eyes,
'Tis writ to counter brazen lies.

THE MAN WITH THE SPATS
(Petrograd, November, 1917)

A MEMORY

How WELL, how well, I remember
Under leaden skies,
That murky night-like day
Of hostile bleakness
Of Peter's dank city
Set in a swamp.

Behold him!—
The man with the spats . . .
Lean and gaunt,
He stands, shivering,
On an ice-clad corner
Of run-down Nevsky,
A forlorn figure
In striped trousers
Immaculately creased,
And black coat
Of good cloth
In bourgeois design,
Yet incongruous
In shabby great-coat
And skull-fitting hat
Of shaggy sheepskin,
Worse for the wear.
And—of all things—
White spats!

Despite formal garb
Of career diplomat
Or prosperous nabob
His face is a mask,
Its name Despair,
Frozen into immobility,
Eyes glazed with misery,
Looking inwardly
Down the years
On a world that was
And is no more,
Fronting, on the brink, the new,
An abyss deep and perilous,
Fraught with dark thoughts
And darker deeds,
Harboring slimy pits
Nesting slithery serpents
Coiled to strike . . .
Groans and lamentations
Are heard
As from an inferno
To stagger Dante. . . .

No Saint George he
To contend with drunken dragon
Run amok,
From forked tongue
Spitting flames of hatred,
Whose loyal minions,
Arms red-beribboned,
Pass by sniggering
At the unmodish sight
Of white hands,
Taper-fingered,
And whiter collar . . .
No longer assets
But dire liabilities . . .

Pathetic he stands
With a bundle of papers
Under his arm . . .
Silent about his wares
Which he must sell
Lest from hunger
His wife and daughter die.
Oh man! You who once sat
In the councils of well-to-do
Of the same Nevsky,
What are your thoughts now?
No matter. "I want a paper, man!
What papers have you?"
The man with the spats
Woke as from a dream.
"Oh, it's you, the Americanetz!
What paper? 'Dead of Night!'" he said,
And smiled grimly.
"What an odd name!" said I
"Not at all," he replied.
"Don't you remember,
A week ago it was 'Dawn!'
The Comrades stepped in,
And it became 'Morn!'
After 'Morn' came 'Noon,'
Then 'Afternoon!'
Then 'twas 'Twilight.'
To be sure 'Evening' followed,
And now it's 'Dead of Night' . . .
A logical sequence. . ." *
Bitterly he smiled.
"What next?" I asked.
"Next? What can be next?
The cock will crow.

---

* This is not a fantasy but an actual fact. Indeed, my copies of the paper with the changing titles, though by no means the entire series, are now in the archives of the Yale University Library.

When he has crowed thrice,
The great betrayal
Will take place,
Who knows—
Perhaps St. Bartholomew's Night . . .
The slaughter of men
With white collars
And even whiter hands . . .
They are quoting Lenin:
'You can't make an omelet
Without breaking eggs . . .'
In the world to come
White collars will be forbidden,
White hands will be tabu . . .
As for spats . . ." he smiled—
"They'll be as dead as dodo! . . .
But there will be omelets
Of human flesh and blood . . ."
"Don't mind my asking," said I,
"What's become of your fine great-coat
Of astrakhan—and smart hat to match?
'Twas but yesterday you wore them!"

He answered:
"You surely have read
Gogol's story 'The Great-coat!'
How the poor chap,
Akaky Akakievich,
Had his great-coat taken
By a couple of hooligans?
Well, now, we Russians have become
A nation of Akakieviches . . .
To make the story short,
Two hoodlooms—one our janitor—
Without much ado walked in
And helped themselves
To my great-coat of astrakhan

And my hat of same . . .
They gave me these . . .
'Out of kindness,' they said.
Then I stood on the landing
And listened to their talk
On the stairs . . .
It was an education,
If a painful one!
They spoke half in rhyme,
Aping slogans,
Proletarian parlance,
In this wise:
'His daughter is a juicy dish,
Too smart to have for father
So poor a fish . . .
Today in her natty togs—
For want of others, poor lass!—
She was clearing the snow,
Shoveling it like you or me.
His wife, too, is a buxom wench,
She may not be a Red,
Yet right jolly in bed . . .
As for him,
The chap in the spats,
What's he to us?
What we to him?
He's had his inning,
His fatted calf.
Are we sorry for him?
Not by half!
Now it's our turn
To eat caviar and larks,
So say Lenin—and Karl Marx!
Yes, it's our turn,
We'll rape and burn . . .
Lenin says all's allowed,

And Lenin is a right smart guy,
Not one to tell us guys a lie . . .
We'll let him have his spats,
Much good they'll do him
When we throw him to the rats!
For a change let the boorjooys
Starve and shrink . . .
What's a revolution for
But to fill our bellies
With food and drink . . .
Expropriate the appropriators
Says that wise guy Lenin . . .
Sure, for this chap
We do not give a rap . . .'
'You've said it, comrade!
His like we'll wipe off the map . . .' . . ."

Suddenly— —
Round the corner
Shots rang out . . .
In a trice
Running bipeds
Hove into view
In avid pursuit
Of a distraught figure
In desperate flight,
Bleeding at the mouth,
Panting as he ran.
Raucous came the cry
In his wake:
"To the canal! Canal!"
There was the rampant echo:
"To the canal with him!
Let's drown the bourgeois scum!"
As if in obedience
To the clamor

Of men eager for his blood
He turned the corner
Into a lane,
Its narrow pavement
Bordering on a canal . . .

The man with the spats
Turned toward me
A face of horror
Frozen into a mask,
Murmuring
When he could speak:
"Poor chap! I knew him well!
Lenin no lion to him . . .
But a Tartar, a killer,
A cruel despot . . .
The Czar had hanged his brother,
So he's turned avenger,
Who'd murder a whole class . . .
Wherefore he is a hero . . .
They see him not
As a demagogue,
A spellbinder,
Speaking from a soap-box
But as a demi-god
Exhorting from a pedestal . . .
In good time, no doubt,
They'll build him a monument,
Worship him
As the Turks' Mohamet . . .
Ere he dies
The land will reek with blood . . .
A curse upon the murderer
And all his kind! . . .
In the name of an Utopia
He will build his Dream

On a graveyard,
Endless with countless corpses . . .
For evil is born of evil,
It lives on . . . and on . . .
To corrupt the generations
Yet to come . . .
Thus it always was
And always thus will be . . ."

Stunned with horror
I felt ill at heart
And fain he'd cease to speak . . .
Yet I was under a compulsive spell
Even as the Wedding Guest,
The Ancient Mariner,
Of the famous poet's story . . .
The man who killed
The Albatross.
I felt buttonholed
And could not help but listen
To a tale whose telling
Seemed to ease the mind
Of the narrator,
Incongruously a man with spats
Which would share in the doom to come . . .
I held up a hand
As a token that I would speak,
But, regardless, he went on:
"You see, such things inure us,
We must learn to suffer
And to endure . . .
We too must pay
For our fathers' sins,
Pay for a foolish Czar,
For his stupider spouse,
For malevolent Rasputin . . ."

Poor chap! He'd have gone on
But for a diversion . . .
A soldier ran
For a passing tram
From whose crowded platform
Men hung on
Like jungle apes
And as he ran
He knocked an old woman down
Who was in his way.
It set some Comrades
Who stood near by
Guffawing . . . What fun!
I took a step
To help the woman up,
But the man with the spats
Restrained me . . .
"Don't!" he cried,
Snatching at my arm . . .
"That's counter-revolution!"
This, with a bitter grin . . .
Indeed, standers-by
In malignant voices mocked:
"Served the old bitch right
To stand in the way
Of a hero of the Revolution!"
Moments passed,
Eternities . . .
By and by a cocky corporal,
A company of twelve,
Judas and his disciples,
Marched by . . .
In grey
With gleaming bayonets
Singing an obscene chastushka*

---

* Chastushka—a popular song, usually on some topic of the day, sung by workers and peasants.

There's no one we need fear,
We can stuff on cheese and beer.
We can take what we do see,
Who'll challenge you or me?

Every laddie has a lance,
Every lassie has her chance,
When her color flushes red
It means it's time to go to bed.

Ha-ha-ha! Ha-ha-ha!
We'll have a jolly tra-la-la!

At the sound of
These strident voices
His face grew pale . . .
On the wing
I caught his thought
Of wife and daughter
Perilled
By this ruthless gentry
Who in the name of Revolution
Had raped a regiment of women
Who bravely defended
The Winter Palace
On the night
Of Lenin's rise to power . . .
A sadder face I'd never seen
Nor hope to see . . .
Mute he stood,
All that words could say
Was in his eyes . . .
The import of their eloquence
Might—and should—
Have moved the world
Which heard the tumult
Of dictators

Despatching orders
From the Smolny,*
Yet who could hear
The silence
Of an aching heart
Against the noisome ardor
Of doctrinnaires
Gone berserk
Over a dubious legacy—
Ideology they called it—
Of an embittered man,
Bees buzzing
In his bushy beard,
Pouring out
Cornucopia-wise
His bitter rancor
With pen dipped
In unadulterated venom,
Bidding men
To exchange chains
Of one tyranny
For those of another
More vexing?
In the name of *vox populi*
They shout,
Worse luck, they shoot.
Their passport to life
Is calloused hands
And—calloused hearts.
Wage war! they shout,
Wage war on class,
Set class against class,
Especially
Against first-class . . .

---

* Smolny Institute—formerly an academy for young women; at this time the official headquarters of the Bolsheviks.

Take what the élite possess
That's good economy
(Thanks to Karl Marx),
But not the precious harvests
Of their brains,
Gathered and matured
Through centuries.
That's contraband!
Burn Raphael
Says their poet,
Renounce Nature,
Glorify the Machine
Pregnant with proletarians
Yet to come.
Above all, "liquidate"
Those who do not agree with you.
A splendid euphemism that
For violent death.

The Man With the Spats
Was "on the spot."
Well he knew it!
My sympathy was his.
What price sympathy
In a Marxian world
Which "liquidates" the very word?
What price compassion?
Love is no more,
Faith is no more,
Their place usurped
By "economic determinism,"
A cold absolute
Sans good will,
Sans neighborliness,
Sans meaning itself!
It is inhuman.
Have you heard a man say

Heartfully,
"Give me economic determinism,
Or give me death!?"
Have you heard a man say
"Be yourself'?"
In a land where
To be oneself
Is a heresy,
Unthinkable,
Unforgivable,
Punishable with death!
Fear lurked in his eyes,
Fear of things impending . . .
And there stood I
In intolerable agony
For inability to help . . .
I shook myself,
Snatched the papers
From under his arm,
Thrust a bill of currency
Into his hand . . .
"For souvenirs!"
I murmured . . .
"Go home, my friend,
Go home, to wife
And daughter . . .
I have an engagement to keep
(I lied)—See you anon!"
Ashamed, off I sped
Into a land
Of restless shadows
Wrapt in mist . . .
Into a land
Of muffled voices
Lost in a wilderness
Of troubled chaos . . .

I pondered:
Where shall I go
To find release
From pent-up feelings?
Where find a refuge
From outraged decency?
A corroding sadness,
All-pervasive,
Possessed me.
With helpless fury
I eyed, overhead,
The hanging placard
Bearing the slogan
"All power to the Soviets!"
The once gay Nevsky,
Plunged in icy mist,
Ever thickening,
Was a thoroughfare
Of diffused horror.
Out of the fog,
Grown denser,
Sinister phantoms
Lurked in doorways
Under granite caryatids,
Whispering,
Or glided by
With stealth,
Their voices sibilant,
Their guffaws obscene,
Leaving a trail
Of perturbation
In their wake . . .
Raucous the cries
Of teenage gamins:
"Pravda!"—"Truth!"
"Izvestia!"—"News!"
Containing all news

Fit to print,
As decreed by Lenin
And his Yes-men . . .

O Dante!
Would that you were here
In this tragic hour
By the new Styx
Called the Neva
With your genial guide
The noble Virgil!
All is falsehood here,
The sign over the door reads:
"Find hope all who enter here!"
A sign to lure
And deceive strangers.
No Beatrice to meet
As the ultimate reward,
But a dubious lady,
Utopia. . . .
Humdrum and remote
Envisioned by one
Whose bushy beard
Gets in one's way,
Whose dull treatise
Is built on a denial
Of Nature and human nature,
On a hope of happiness attained
By the conversion
Of human beings
Into a race of robots,
Of submissive cogs
Manipulating automata . . .
O Dante!
Mellifluous poet
Who once dwelt
So unhappily

On the torments of the damned . . .
Come . . gaze at the prejudged . . .
With contiguous,
Unmitigated pity,
Observe the tragic spectacle,
Listen to the torments
Of the hapless stricken,
To the laments of innocents
Snared with the guilty . . .
Pray render manifest
To a world agog,
A world credulous
And incredulous,
The whole, the bare truth,
Anent a monstrous lie
Foisted on humanity . . .
Tell it with the tragic beauty
Of living images . . .

I trudged on,
Pausing here and there,
To gaze at the tiny chapels
Which dotted the Nevsky.
Lighted tapers within,
They were oases of light . . .
You saw a lone worshipper,
Sometimes more,
Kneeling before an image lamp
Illumining an ikon
Of saint or Virgin,
Murmuring a prayer . . .
Suddenly I heard a keening.
Lifting my eyes,
I beheld, approaching,
A host of women,
Hundreds of them . . .

Beshawled peasants,
Poorly apparelled,
A motley procession . . .
Grave-faced,
They marched,
Intoning a dirge-like chant . . .
Made a sign of the cross,
Murmuring the while:
"*Gospody, pomilooy!*"—
"O Lord, have mercy on us!"
Above their heads
Sacred banners, red and gold,
Were swinging.
A cassocked priest
Marched in the lead,
Beside him four acolytes,
Censers in their hands
Emitting fumes of incense . . .
They cried to the heavens
Their heart-felt laments . . .
They bemoaned the fate
That overtook
"Little Mother Russia,"
Sought to exorcise
The newly-risen Antichrist
In their midst . . .

The procession moved on . . .
Passed out of mind . . .
When, suddenly,
A ray of the sun
Clove the fog,
Shone kindly
On my bemused mind,
Opening vistas of memory . . .
'Twas then I bethought myself

Of a friend,
An old man,
A scholar . . .
A man of parts,
Who possessed great treasure,
A roomful of books,
Friends perennially loyal . . .
I'll look in on him.
Perhaps at the sight
Of these repositories
Of lore and wisdom,
Rich as dusty bottles are
In old wine,
I may regain
A litle of my cheer,
Renew my spirit
At the fount of a fine mind,
The mind of my friend . . .
Good fortune attending,
I found him at home.
In response to my knock
He opened the door . . .
Silently—
With unaccustomed gravity,
He led me along the corridor
To the room he knew I loved
Above all rooms . . .

Horrors!—
With feelings akin to despair
I gazed at empty shelves
Where ten thousand steadfast friends
Shoulder to shoulder
Had once reposed . . .
From wall to wall,
From floor to ceiling,
There now gaped at me

Yards of shelves
Bereft of their treasure
They had formerly,
So proudly tenanted....
I gazed at the patriarch
With snow-white beard,
Awaited an explanation....
He looked at me
With eyes intelligent and kind,
A faint hint of a smile
Graced them,
A blend of irony and sadness...
Suddenly, in a manner abrupt,
He laughed...
Had the old man gone daft?
"What is the meaning?" I asked.
"Meaning?" he echoed,
"You ask that?...
You might have guessed...
It was but yesterday
The 'comrades' were here
And bore my books away in carts...
'Nationalized,' my friend!"
At first I was speechless,
Then burst into loudness:
"Saints alive!...
Donnerwetter!...
Great Jehoshaphat!...
O God, O Montreal!...
Hell's bells!..."
He gazed at me benignly.
"You're astonished, my friend, I see—
And indignant...!"
"With good reason!" I replied.
"You gathered these books
Through endless years,

Spent on them your sustenance,
And, building on them,
Have written many books
For the glory of Russia,
To spread her fame
Among the nations,
So that the whole earth
From pole to pole
Might know
What a great heart,
And great soul,
Had given birth
To Pushkin and to Gogol,
To Tolstoy and Dostoevsky,
To Borodin and to Scriabin,
To Glinka and Moussorgsky . . .
What now, my friend,
That the tools of your trade
Have been stolen from you?"
Serene my friend's smile
As he made response . . .
Serene, too, his voice:
"I welcomed the Revolution
When it first came
On that marvellous day
In March . . .
Was it not the great men
Whose august names
You've just recited,
And others like them,
Who gave the original impetus,
The primal urge,
To the great event,
Who suffered and endured
That the free Slav spirit
Might exult? . . .

When that day came
I thought my work was done . . .
With a full heart
And high spirits
I greeted that memorable day
In March . . .
And now it's November,
Spring is no more,
Summer is gone too . . .
Their warmth
And softness
Have gone out of life . . .
The Revolution
Is in the winter of its soul,
It bodes ill for us . . .
It was ever thus . . .
I erred in thinking
This was different . . .
Yesterday morning
When the Comrades came
To remove my books,
The eternally faithful,
The eternally beloved
Companions of my life,
I saw myself for what I was . . .
A soft-hearted Girondist
Yielding my dearest possessions,
My very heart,
To the intrepid Jacobins
Who let me, helplessly, look on
While they stripped my shelves . . .
Not they to stand
Foolishness and nonsense.
They did but follow
The natural law of Revolution:
'Expropriate the expropriators!'

'Property is theft!' they quoted
Proudhon—and Karl Marx . . .
And yet, my friend,
Could it have been different?
Not human beings they—
Not any longer . . .
But Abstractions,
Absolutes,
Cogwheels in the machine
Of violence . . .
What can you expect?
Theirs the law of have-nots . . .
For so very long
Society has kept them
On the leash
In sight of food
And fine clothes
And books . . .
They might look at these
But not possess . . .
This is a storm, my friend,
A storm of human wrath
Which minds not
What it sweeps
Out of its way . . .
They took my books
And left me living . . .
Have you heard
What happened
This very day? . . .
No? . . . . Well . . . listen . . .
Red sailors
Of the Kronstadt fleet
Made the rounds of hospitals
And slain three fine men
In their beds . . .

Good revolutionaries
They were too . . .
But not of the Lenin brand!
Not Lenin the man
To balk at spilling of blood . . .
He has lodged in jail
His own best friend,
Menshevik Plekhanov,
A better wiser man than he!
The reason?—Simple!
Plekhanov balked at violence,
Advocated peaceful means,
Favored evolution . . .
Yet the people
Needed no urging—
No, not from Lenin . . .
They'd suffered long denial,
The mother of greed.
'Twas not long since
They'd often passed
The opulent window
Of the Elisseyev shop
On the Nevsky.
That window flaunted
Barrels of caviar,
Both red and black,
Not one barrel, my friend,
But three—or even four . . .
Mammoth barrels!
Yes, and other goodies, too,
In generous measure . . .
At any rate, enough
To fire men to fury,
To drive them,
Now that chance offers,
To ruthlessness. . . ."

I interrupted,
Told him of the plight
Of the man with the spats,
Of my concern for him.
What will happen? I asked.
His eyes filmed with pity,
He threw up his hands
In a futile gesture.
"That is sad, very sad,"
He murmured . . .
"For him 'tis harder
Than for me . . .
I am old,
My wife is dead,
I have some fame . . .
Having done no harm,
They'll pass me by . . .
I am known abroad . . .
They will not risk
Needless displeasure
Of foreign folk
Who honor me . . .
But that poor man,
Your man with spats,
It may go hard with him.
He is one of many
Without a place
In a Communist paradise,
He is, so I fear,
An expendable . . ."

"True," I agreed,
"There's the pity!
Sans a worker's blood,
A passport to Red favor,
Sans fame,
He can but rot in jail,

Die by a bullet
Or starvation . . .
Without memories
While he lives,
Unremembered when he dies . . .
Guiltless,
Defenceless,
A good husband,
A good father—
Virtues of no account,
A white collar
And uncalloused hands,
Detriments,
He has no status,
He can count on nothing.
His the most tragic lot of all!
Fated, perhaps, to become
An ingredient
In the Marx-Lenin omelet!
An American,
Citizen of a free country,
My blood boils
At the very thought,
Of the indignity inflicted
On any man at the mercy
Of ruthless tyrants
Who may manhandle
As they will,
Without a soul
To murmur protest! . . ."

By now exhausted
By my own tirade,
By my passion,
Futile in the face
Of a hurricane

Of unbridled wrath
Cruel to one and all
Who face it
In a spirit of combat,
I grew speechless
For the tears
Who struggled
In my throat . . .
Ruefully he smiled,
His eyes compassionate:
"You have a warm heart . . .
In our time a warm heart
Is a liability.
I must confess:
To hide my aches
And ease my soul
I take comfort
In the written word . . .
Poetry, music, art,
Are my solace.
Poetry above all.
Now in my dotage
I even write it . . .
An old dream come to life.
This very day
I've penned some verse,
In imitation
Of English nonsense rhyme
I've learned to admire.
It's a simple piece
Writ in the English tongue
More fitting for this than our own.
We Russians are a solenm folk,
Tiomnye Liudi—'a dark people'
We have been called . . .
Forgive an old man's vanity,

I'll read it to you,
It's best merit
Is its brevity . . ."
From an inner pocket
He drew a sheet of paper
And read:
>   *"I am an old man,*
>   *An old man am I,*
>   *Though I am three score*
>   *—and more*
>   *I feel gay and spry.*
>   *The reason is not far to seek,*
>   *Not far to seek at all,*
>   *For I am an old man*
>   *And not afraid to die."*

I was about to speak,
He would not have me.
He thrust the sheet
Into my hand, and said:
"A poor thing,
Yet take it,
As a souvenir,
As a memento
Of this final hour,
Before you return to your own,
Your happier land . . ."
Abruptly
He strode toward
A corner of the room,
Now bare of books,
And put a record
On an old machine . . .
The Second Movement
Of Beethoven's *Seventh* . . .
It was his favorite,
Mine, too . . .

Rapt, we listened,
He made the comment:
"I saw your countrywoman,
Isadora Duncan,
Dance this on our Russian stage,
I thought then as now:
Here is German music,
An American dancer,
A Russian audience ...
An English conductor—Coates,
This is as should be,
Beauty is universal,
It knows no boundaries,
'Tis art, 'tis love, 'tis faith.
'Tis a woman loving a man,
A man loving a woman,
'Tis a mother nursing her child,
'Tis the Good Samaritan
Coming to the aid
Of the afflicted.
Above all, 'tis love,
'Tis a tender passion
Expressed in paint,
In words,
In sound.
There is love, beauty,
In your Lincoln's
Exquisite prose poem,
The Gettysburg address ...
'Twas our own Dostoevsky
Who said rightly,
'Beauty will save the world.'
It alone unites,
All the rest separates.
We shall drift
Into a new darkness here ...

A domain of tooth and claw . . .
Men shall do evil
In the name of good.
But Europe lives in me . . .
Here, amid the coming terror,
I shall put on old records
On the old machine . . .
And the sweet poison
Of the West
Shall pour out of this circling disc
And fill me with the old ecstasy . . .
It will save me
From the pain of betrayal . . .
Yes . . . betrayal . . .
Even by friend and kin . . ."
His voice quavered . . .
His pallor deepened . . .

"I'll tell you a secret,"
He hoarsely whispered.
"Do you know why I am bereft
Of my friends, my books,
My army of counsellors,
Ten thousand in number?
My sister—my own sister,
Varvara—you've met her,
A fanatical apostle
Of Marx and Lenin,
She spent here hour upon hour,
Expostulating, arguing,
Gesticulating with her hands,
In an endeavor to convert me
To the cause of the Soviets.
I told her I approved
Their ultimate ideal
But could not countenance,

Their *modus operandi,*
Their bent for violence.
I feared their means
Would terminate
In becoming their end.
I pleaded—all to no avail.
She was adamant
In her eyes
I was a heretic.
Vain my pleading . . .
I told her, too,
I loved her dearly,

That I would not,
Indeed I could not
Join a movement
Repugnant to mind and heart . . .
Why not remain as we were,
I pleaded,
She a believer,
I a skeptic . . .
We were brother and sister,
We could remain friends . . .
But no! . . .
As a loyal Red, she said,
She could, would not,
Let matters rest . . .
She knew they were after my books,
She had the power
To let me keep what was mine
During my lifetime.
But as things were
She would not hinder
Her taskmasters
From stripping me
Of my cherished friends.
I could keep them

Only at the price
Of unconditional surrender . . .
She left in a huff . . .
You see, these men
Recognize no natural law:
Mother, sister, brother,
Son or daughter,
Convey no meaning
Except as friends or enemies
Of the Cause . . .
They know no neutrals . . .
Now you know . . ."

I stood there aghast
At the revelation
Of such base betrayal
From one's own blood . . .
I wished to speak,
But could not . . .
He saw my plight . . .
"Listen to the music," said he,
"The magic of Beethoven
Reconciles one even to betrayal,
Lifts us above all sordid things,
Softens horror,
Repels hatred
To let love enter in . . .
Don't fret, my friend,
On my account . . .
This, too, shall pass . . .
Human nature will triumph.
In the meanwhile
There is music . . .
I shall live as always—
Myself and unafraid. . . ."

As the strains of Beethoven
Died away
There was pathos,
Weariness,
In his noble face . . .
An unutterable sadness.
"Come," said I,
"Come to America with me,
You are a man of repute,
You can plead for asylum,
They'll welcome you . . ."
"No, no, my friend!
That can never be,
I draw my sap of life
From my native soil . . .
Even in travail
Russia is infinitely dear to me.
Here was I born,
Here grew and throve,
Here I stay . . ."
Twilight was falling
When I left him . . .
We'd embraced
And without needless word
We parted . . .
Twilight was falling,
Embraced me
In a mood of troubled dream,
As I wended my way
Toward my lodging
Close by . . .
The front doors
Were barred
Against intruders,
So I turned to the archway
To the left,
Opening on a courtyard.

In answer to my ring,
The janitor,
A morose fellow,
Opened the gate,
And muttered:
"Ah, we Russians
Are a dark folk . . .
Again the electricity
Is cut off,
The lift's not running . . .
Too bad, *barin,*
But you'll have to climb
The dark back stairs . . .
Time's not what it used to be . . ."
I thrust a couple of Kerenskys*
Into his expectant hand
And entered a narrow door
And began my climb
On the narrower stair,
Which at intervals spiralled.
It was dark,
I had no flashlight,
I groped my way
By feeling along the wall.
On the fifth story at last,
With more groping
With by now accustomed hands
I unlocked the door,
And entered a dark,
None too large chamber.
I groped for a candle . . .
Lighting it,
I found a cold frugal supper
Laid out by the landlady,
A good woman, bereaved of husband,

---

* Kerenskys were the name given to the paper currency during the Kerensky regime.

A cavalryman in the Tsar's army
Slain in the big war . . .

She had a boy of fourteen,
Meager of build,
His eyes blinking
From malnutrition . . .
He had been destined
For the school of cadets;
This hope was gone.
Only the other day
What cadets there were
Died at the hands of Reds
While defending
The last Tsarist stronghold
In which they'd gathered.
They died gallantly.
The son of an officer,
The landlady's son
Had a mark against him
By that circumstance.
Poor lad,
Your eyes blinking
Like a neon light,
There's none to help you,
None to pity you . . .
When I am gone
There'll be less to eat.
To feed and shelter you,
Your mother will go selling
Souvenirs left by your father
In the Black Market . . .
His pistols at least
Will fetch a goodly price,
And his half dozen razors
Of tempered steel

Made in Germany
And in Sheffield
Will find a buyer
In some well-to-do Red nabob,
Who, moreover,
May discover
A not too elusive charm
In your mother.
That's the way of the world, my lad,
In Red Russia
As in Imperial Rome . . .
The lady is comely . . .
The friendly Commissar
May even endeavor
For her sake
To enroll you
In the Soviet youth . . .

But enough . . . enough . . .
Weary in soul and body
From the day's ordeal,
I flung myself
Upon the cot.
Somnolent,
Yet I could not sleep.
Unhappy thoughts
Jostled one another,
Restless, they contended,
Raced in wild profusion,
Feverish moments,
Precipitate,
Stumbled on one another
Pell-mell fashion . . .
I craved sleep,
Forgetfulness,
Oblivion . . .

I was jolted within,
Bidden to rise,
Challenged to fare forth
Into the mad turmoil
Of that dark addled cosmos
Of a new world
In the making.
Unmindful of night,
Of perils lurking
In the shape
Of shapeless forms
Inhabiting the mist
Which sought victims
Among hapless passers-by
And bystanders,
I could not if I would
Refuse the imperative summons . . .

Girding my loins,
As the Good Book says,
I ventured forth
On my nocturnal pilgrimage . . .
A perilous journey.
I found myself walking
Among shadows,
Among ghosts of eras past,
Prowlers insubstantial,
Forms intangible,
Impalpable,
Mere mobile blurs,
Meaningless smudges
On a painter's canvas . . .
They formed and reformed
Fantastically
Before my eyes
In the dense fog
Shot through with shafts

Of Northern lights . . .
The eerie glare
Mingled with the dusk
To my confusion . . .
Like a sleepwalker
I ambled on
In aimless fashion,
Dubious, irresolute,
Beset by corrosive forces
Charged with opiates,
Inducing lassitude.
Who was I? What was I?
A phantom among phantoms?
A wraith among shadows?
A shadow of a shade?
An animated automaton
Endowed with blind impulsion?
A disembodied spirit
Lost in envenomed cloud
Explosive in substance?
No question here of
"To be, or not to be,"
But one of
"Am I, or am I not?"
A question insoluble.
I was a lambent being
Drifting in irreality,
Irrevocably lost
In some formless Inferno,
Maze of nameless horror.
A serpent,
Quicksilvery, slippery,
Voicing a slender sibilance,
Slithered at will,
Sinuously,
Through the countless convolutions
Of my supine brain,

Leaving chills of dread
In its repulsive trail,
A lingering sense
Of impending doom . . .
Like a sharp saber
Reposing in scabbard,
My live soul lay still
Within my body . . .
I plunged deeper
Into the shadows . . .

Before I knew it
I stood in an open square,
And there,
Fronting me,
Was the Bronze Horseman,
Peter, surnamed the Great,
Founder of the city
He had built with loving care
On soil he had won in battle.
I saw the famous silhouette
But faintly . . .
A passing cloud of mist
Hid the rider from sight
But left in sharp outline
The rearings forelegs
Of the wild steed
Straining at the reins . . .

I would fain
Have approached nearer,
When suddenly I espied
Two moving silhouettes
Below the fore-hooves.
I discerned in one
A bushy beard,
In the other

A pendent pigtail . . .
Who were they?
I was soon to know.
For presently I heard
The sound of voices . . .
A dialogue ensued
Of which I shall here attempt
To give the substance.

"What luck to find you,
Mister Karl Marx!
I thought you'd be around.
I knew you at once
By your celebrated beard . . .
A beard is thought by some
To be a sign of wisdom . . .
Yours has a strange resemblance
To a broom—a new broom
Which sweeps clean . . .
It has done that,
I must own to it . . ."
"And who are you, pray?"
Inquired a guttural voice
With a teutonic intonation.
"I?" said the other,
"I thought you wouldn't know me . . .
But you've heard of me, I'm sure . . .
I too, in my time,
Have swept things clean
In my own fashion . . .
I am Genghis Khan . . ."
"What can Genghis Khan
Have to say to me—
To Karl Marx? . . .
We speak a different language,
It would seem . . ."
Genghis Khan laughed,

111

It was a genial guffaw,
As he made reply:
"It only seems so,
Mister Karl Marx,
But not really,
As presently
I shall demonstrate . . .
We are both killers.
'Perfect Warrior'
Is the meaning of my name.
At the head of the so-called
Golden Hordes,
Armies of Mongols,
I swept over Russia,
Slaying thousands upon thousands,
And made the rest
Pay handsome tribute
To fill and re-fill my treasury,
We did our slaying
In the good old honest way,
With saber, bow and lance . . .
What difference between us,
Between you and me?
A fair question!
The answer:
You are doing the killing
With a book! . . .
Our methods are different,
The result is the same . . .
Your harvest of killing
Is still before you.
The Russian soil
Will reek with blood
Ere you are done!"
"So you, Genghis Khan,
Have read *Das Kapital!*"

There was satisfaction
In Marx's voice.
"What do you think of it?"
"Me read *Das Kapital?*"
Returned the Mongol.
"No, not me! Books bore me,
Unless they have a hero
Who makes mincemeat of other chaps
When he is so minded . . .
I do not like statistics,
Economic data
And that sort of thing . . .
Don't ask me to read your book,
It's the results that count.
The men who will do the killing
Will not be the men
Who have read your book . . .
The Lenins and the Trotskys
Sit pretty . . .
Sending out orders
In your name . . .
I, Genghis Khan, approve,
And must confess:
Your words
Transmitted to underlings
Do the work of slaying
As well as my sabers,
Bows and lances,
Ever did!
You're a smart one . . .
It is due to your eminence
As a prospective killer
On an expansive scale,
That I've come a long way
To seek you out.
I have a proposition

> To make to you
> Along your own line.
> Ere I mention it
> I wish to note:
> You and I are realists,
> So let's eschew poetics
> And have our say in prose."

"That's okay by me, as the Yanks would say, Mister Genghis Khan. Proceed—in prose!"

"See this statue?"

"I have eyes."

"But you may not see what I see!"

"What is it that's denied me?"

"We can go far together—you and I. Or rather you can go far—with my help."

"Didn't know you were a philanthropist, Mister Genghis Khan!"

"Maybe not. I stand to gain by it, too."

"To the point, please!"

"Be patient, my friend. We'll get farther that way. After all, Mister Marx, it took you a million words or thereabouts to explain your idea to the world. Now I am a man of action, and will not subject you to so uncomfortable an ordeal . . . To come to the point, then, I suggest you unseat this fellow Peter, and take his place in the saddle. The horse, as you know, is Russia. It is a refractory horse. It's rearing to go, to kick over the traces. Here's your chance to ride roughshod over all of Russia—possibly the world. That's where I'll come in—with heavy reinforcements!"

"Before we go on with this, Mister Genghis Khan, I wish to remark that I have a soft spot for this Peter. Were it not for him I might not be here now. I owe a debt to him!"

"A debt? How can that be . . . Gratitude, I always understood, was considered a bourgeois virtue."

"Well, you see, when Peter built this city on soil he conquered from the Swedes, it was with the idea of making it a window on Europe.' You must know what I mean. He wanted Western culture to steal through that window. That gave me a chance. For all my bulk, I slithered through it, with *Das Kapital* under my arm. It was a tough job getting through with that contraband. Well, thanks to Peter, here I am!"

"Exactly, here you are. With one foot in the stirrup, too! To speak the truth, I didn't expect you to be sentimental about Peter. He didn't put this window here for the sakes of you! Indeed he'd have thought twice about it if he knew it would bring you here, and you know it!"

"I see your point. There's something in that!"

"To be sure. Indeed, I may also point out that your disciples here aren't so squeamish. And it won't surprise me a bit if they should rename this city after one of their own chaps. Maybe even after you!"

"Do you really think so?"

"No matter. I know one person they will not name it after. Even though Genghisgrad wouldn't sound a bit bad! And not unjust either. When my armies were here they laid many a native woman. I vow, there's not a little Mongol blood in the Russians. My distinguished fellow conqueror, Napoleon, wasn't so far from the truth when he said: 'Scratch a Russian, and find a Tartar!'"

"You make a point there! . . . . But this is not a debating society!"

"You're bloody right there, Mister Karl Marx! . . . Let's clear the air a bit. The world has an idea that Russia is a Sphinx. Where, actually, Russia is the rearing horse here, waiting only for a chance to kick up and ride roughshod over things. And you, a rank foreigner, started all that. Now here is your chance. Mount that horse, and leave it to him to leave drippings behind as he gallops across the length and breadth of the land. But only with you in the saddle, holding the reins!"

"But I've never ridden a horse, my friend!"

"Don't worry about that. I was in the old days a wild rider. And I conquered Russia riding at the head of my army. I am still a good rider. I'll sit behind you. And, anyhow, we'll be invisible. We are dead, you know. But our souls will go marching on! Together on this spirited horse we'll ride roughshod over the Capitalist world, according to your desire. In the result you'll first have all of Russia, then Europe, then maybe—maybe—England and America—

"Ah, you've touched a sort spot, my friend. I thought the Revolution would begin in England, so full of ready-made proletarians. That it should have started in this backward country was something of a disappointment to me. I am sorry to have to confess I was a poor prophet on that score. As for America, it was beyond my dreams. It's so full of capitalists whom it would be nice to destroy. Anyhow, how can a horse cross an ocean?"

"Ah, you disappoint me, Karl Marx! We'll go on a ship of course! We are invisible. We are ideas! We shall need no passports. We shan't need this horse either. They have fast trains there. They have them in England, too. Nothing so primitive as this. That reminds me. How did it come about that they let you live so much of your life in England while you were England's enemy, plotting to destroy her?"

"How ignorant you are, Mister Genghis Khan! They have free speech there. You can get up on the soap box there in Hyde Park, in the very heart of London, and talk against the English system to your heart's content. Why, they even put policemen at your disposal to protect you against anyone who doesn't like your talk and would like to punch your nose for you! They are a strange people, the English!"

"Strange indeed, Mister Karl Marx! And you don't feel any gratitude for the shelter they gave you? But a little while ago, you were a bit squeamish about your debt to Peter!"

"That's different, my friend! They liked to have me here, just to show how liberal they were—how little afraid they were of anyone who contested their ideas! They thought they were the only people in the world worth their salt. They took it for granted, too, that the whole world knew it! It would be a real pleasure to pull the British lion's tail!"

"What you tell me surprises me greatly, Mister Karl Marx . . . But we have gotten off the track. I was about to offer you the biggest prize of all, when we went off on a tangent. You like big numbers, statistics, data, and that sort of thing, don't you?"

"To be sure, they are my food and drink! If you had read *Das Kapital*, you'd have known it. But what's this wonderful prize you have in mind?"

"Now we come to the root of the matter. To my part in this vast undertaking. It will take years of work . . . To come to the point, I offer you China! On a silver platter, my friend!"

"Have I heard you all right? You offer me what?"

"China, I said. Six hundred million Mongols who, in good time, will swear by you, work for you, conquer for you. A reservoir of men worth considering, eh? And what if we lose three hundred million of them in the fight! A mere bagatelle . . . We can afford it!"

"Your proposition is *kolossal!*"

"I am glad you are beginning to see the light! With that number of people we can overrun the world, you supplying the idea, I the drive. We'll establish the Marxist Empire . . ." The speaker chuckled.

"I am speechless . . ."

"Admit it: for the first time!"

"Please don't jest about it. It's a big, a serious idea!"

"To be sure it is. Yet permit me a single jest, a serious jest. I think it was you who taught Lenin the notion that you can't make an omelet without breaking eggs!"

117

"Yes, I think I may take credit for it!"

"Well, I am going to complete that jest for you. Yo[u] are Caucasians. You are white. We are Mongols. We a[re] yellow. As you know, no omelet is all white. There is ye[l]low in it. Ah, this is where we Mongols come in. We'[ll] supply the yolks in the omelet! . . . Ha! Ha! Ha! We—you and I—working together—will make a colossal om[e]let—an omelet to end all omelets! Ha! Ha! Ha!"

"Ha! Ha! Ha! . . . But won't there be too much yo[lk] for the white?"

"By no means—for you have the whole white world t[o] draw on!"

"But remember, it's capitalists, exploiters, the drones w[e] are going to dispose of, not the proletarians!"

"Of course, I'm with you there. Yet you must conced[e] that we must kill those proletarians who oppose Commu[]nism. Even now in this Russia there are many such!"

"I fear you are right, Mister Genghis Khan!"

> The bargain sealed
> With a handshake
> That made Marx wince,
> The brutish Mongol,
> Down on his haunches,
> Sprang into action,
> Into a mad squat dance,
> A frenzied whirl,
> While the author of *Das Kapital*
> Watched with civilized disdain,
> Musing on the uncomfortable fact
> That one must put up
> With violence,
> Brutality,
> Savagery,
> Of bestial men,
> To achieve ideal ends . . .

When suddenly—
The dancer rose to his feet,
Exclaiming,
"There is a dead man here,
Doubtless one of your early victims,
Mister Karl Marx,
A gentleman by the look of him,
Maybe a Capitalist—
And look!
What's on his ankles?"
Karl Marx peered down.
"Well, if it isn't spats!
A venerable English institution,
A symbol of gentility,
In short, a bourgeois man
Par excellence!
That's what the land
Of Shakespeare
Has come to!
Shakespeare's day
Was long ago . . .
He dipped his pen
Into the ink-bottle,
Created verbal fantasies,
Made magic music
Out of words . . .
The time for that is past,
I dipped my pen
Into the same ink-bottle
And pulled out a time bomb
Whose moment to explode
Is nigh . . .
It is my special
And particular goal
To terminate the class
Which flaunts

White hands,
White collars,
And white spats . . .
They are the exploiters
Of those who hold such things
In utter contempt . . .
They are of the class
I wish to see destroyed . . ."
"Leave that to me,"
Said Genghis Khan,
"Red blood will flow . . ."

I listened to the speeches
Of these two,
Who had become as one,
With bursting rage,
Bitterness welled up in me
With a force not to be stayed . . .
I wanted to shout,
I wanted my words to be heard
In the troubled Cosmos:
"Freemen of the world, unite!
Unite and fight,
If you would not acquire chains!"
But no words came
Out of my parched throat . . .
It was then I awoke
Out of my nightmare,
Bathed in copious sweat . . .
There was a knock on the door.
It was my landlady . . .
"Are you in pain?" she asked.
"I heard you cry out,
Thought you might be ill,
In a delirium of fever . . ."
" 'Twas a nightmare!" I said.

"Tea—or coffee, sir?"
"Coffee," said I,
"And make it black!"

That morning
I ventured out
On the Nevsky,
To the familiar corner . . .
The Man With the Spats
Was not there . . .
Not there—not there . . .
I went again
On the next day,
And the next . . .
He was not there—not there . . .
Thinking of my dream,
I was as one bereft . . .
Somewhere
From the deep within
Unthought . . .
Unbidden . . .
Came the words,
Uttered aloud:
"Lord have mercy on your soul,
Lord have mercy on the souls
Of those—a multitude of souls—
Soon to die! . . ."

Postscript

This is my story,
Alas, 'tis true,
A tale sans glory,
For me, for you.

It did relieve
My mind to tell it.
You must believe,
I here re-live it . . .

"THE END IS MY BEGINNING"

I hear it still,
The sighing of the pines,
The endless song of tree-tops,
That eternal rustle
In Ukrainian forest
Where I was born and bred
And lived a lonely childhood,
My eyes on sunny days
Joying in the not-too-distant cupolas of Kieff,
Gleaming gold and silver . . .

This was oh so long ago;
Seven decades, and more,
Have passed since I have seen it last,
And I have seen the world
Which has seen upheavals
And survived,
Even as I have,
Yet that song
In the fathomless depths of memory
And of heart
Persists . . .

Nothing, nothing, can still it.
Memory brings back:
The tiny village,
Peasant-tenanted,
Simple folk who abode
In thatch-roofed hovels,
And on festive days,
To strains of concertina,

Danced out-of-doors
On the green sward,
The trepak and the squat,
Now singly, now paired,
Lusty men and youths
With lusty women and girls,
These shawl-bedecked,
Their multi-colored skirts
And petticoats
In kaleidoscopic movement
Permitting snatches for the eyes
Of sturdy nakedness
Above the half-length boots,
The men and women looking on
Clapping their hands in unison
In rhythm . . .

But mostly on sunny days
I spent my hours in the woods . . .
Oft in grass-clad glade
I lay on my back,
The sun in my face,
The breathing warm earth beneath,
Both soothing . . .
Reposing thus,
I listened to the steady rhythmic rustle
Of pliant tree-tops
Swaying in the breeze,
To the accompaniment of birds' twitter . . .

Ten such years of childhood
Have I spent in this simple wise . . .
There was,
With encircling porch,
The large frame house
In which we lived . . .

I still remember
The pungent smell of fresh-baked bread,
Whose crusts, while still hot,
My sisters and I craved and fought for,
Crusts, which when buttered,
Tasted to us young
Better than ambrosia
Could have tasted to the gods!

And now, decades later,
I abide in the biggest
Noisiest city in the world . . .
I hear its tumultuous racket,
Which I cannot shut out—
The ringing of church bells,
The tooting of taxi horns,
The prolonged alarms
Of sirens of fire-engines
And hospital ambulances
Rushing headlong through the night,
The intermittent tremor of subway in my flat,
The endless roll of trucks,
The raucous voices of loud-speakers
Proclaiming the merits
Of this or that candidate
In election to come . . .
And worst of all
On hot days
The rock-drills
Boring holes in the pavement
To get at faulty drains . . .
Or ear-splitting bulldozers
Operating on steel girders
To add one more babel
To multitude of babels . . .
Then again through open window

The softer clamor
Of neighboring radio or gramophone
Asserting the claim for fame
Of some noisy soprano
Or of an ambitious bass
Emulating Chaliapin . . .

I hear all this—and more,
Yet all these multitudinous rampant noises
Do not drown out
The remembered quiet song of childhood . . .
In my heart I hear it still:
Those trees in Ukrainian forest
In sight of ancient holy Kieff
Pining, sighing, rustling,
Through eternity.

Night of January 29, 1963.